TRAILBLAZERS
of the MODERN WORLD

MAHATMA GANDHI

By Ann Heinrichs

WORLD ALMANAC® LIBRARY

Please visit our web site at: www.worldalmanaclibrary.com
For a free color catalog describing World Almanac® Library's list of high-quality books
and multimedia programs, call 1-800-848-2928 (USA) or 1-800-461-9120 (Canada).
World Almanac® Library's Fax: (414) 332-3567.

Library of Congress Cataloging-in-Publication Data

Heinrichs, Ann.
    Mahatma Gandhi / by Ann Heinrichs.
       p. cm. — (Trailblazers of the modern world)
    Includes bibliographical references and index.
    Summary: A biography of the Indian political and spiritual leader who furthered a strategy of nonviolent civil
disobedience to coerce Britain into granting independence to India in 1947.
    ISBN 0-8368-5064-5 (lib. bdg.)
    ISBN 0-8368-5224-9 (softcover)
    1. Gandhi, Mahatma, 1869-1948—Juvenile literature. 2. India—Politics and government—1919-1947—Juvenile
literature. 3. Statesmen—India—Biography—Juvenile literature. 4. Nationalists—India—Biography—Juvenile
literature. [1. Gandhi, Mahatma, 1869-1948. 2. Statesmen. 3. India—Politics and government—1919-1947.]
I. Title. II. Series.
DS481.G3H43   2001
954.03'5'092—dc21
    [B]   2001034141

This North American edition first published in 2001 by
World Almanac® Library
330 West Olive Street, Suite 100
Milwaukee, WI 53212 USA

This U.S. edition © 2001 by World Almanac® Library.

An Editorial Directions book
Editor: Lucia Raatma
Designer and page production: Ox and Company
Photo researcher: Dawn Friedman
Indexer: Timothy Griffin
Proofreader: Neal Durando
World Almanac® Library art direction: Karen Knutson
World Almanac® Library editor: Jacqueline Laks Gorman
World Almanac® Library production: Susan Ashley and Jessica L. Yanke

Photo credits: Hulton/Archive/Hulton Getty/Elliot & Fry, cover; Hulton/Archive/Hulton Getty/Fox Photos, 4;
Hulton/Archive/Hulton Getty, 5; Hulton/Archive/Hulton Getty/E.O. Hoppe, 6; Hulton/Archive/Hulton Getty/The
Statesman Calcutta, 7; AP/Wide World Photos, 8; Corbis/Tiziana and Gianni Baldizzone, 9 top; Hulton/Archive/Hulton
Getty, 9 bottom; AP/Wide World Photos, 10; Hulton/Archive/Hulton Getty/International Feature Service, 11;
Hulton/Archive/Hulton Getty, 12, 13; AP/Wide World Photos, 14; Hulton/Archive/Hulton Getty, 15, 16; Corbis/Hulton-
Deutsch Collection, 17; Hulton/Archive/Hulton Getty, 18–19, 21; Hulton/Archive/Express Newspapers, 22; AP/Wide
World Photos, 23; Hulton/Archive/Hulton Getty, 24; Hulton/Archive/Hulton Getty/Walter Bosshard, 26;
Hulton/Archive/Popperfoto, 27; Corbis/Hulton-Deutsch Collection, 28; AP/Wide World Photos, 29; Corbis/Hulton-Deutsch
Collection, 30; Hulton/Archive/Hulton Getty, 31, 32; AP/Wide World Photos, 33; Hulton/Archive/Hulton Getty, 35, 36, 37;
AP/Wide World Photos, 38, 39, 40, 41; AP/Wide World Photos/Kuni Takahashi, 42 top; Hulton/Archive/Reuters/Peter
Andrews, 42 bottom; Corbis/Bettmann, 43.

Printed in the United States of America

1 2 3 4 5 6 7 8 9 05 04 03 02 01

TABLE of CONTENTS

CHAPTER 1

THE MAN WHO WOULD NOT FIGHT

Mohandas Karamchand Gandhi didn't look very important. He was small and thin, and his voice was shy and quiet. People who passed him on the street wouldn't have noticed him at all. Yet this humble, soft-spoken man turned out to be one of the most powerful and influential leaders in history. People all over the world watched him, listened to his message, and decided to change their lives.

Gandhi's ideas about nonviolence changed the lives of many people.

THE GIFT OF NONVIOLENCE

Gandhi is known as the "Father of India." After a lifetime of working for human rights, he led the people of India to independence in 1947. But his greatest gift to the world was an idea—nonviolence. He believed in solving problems peacefully, without fighting. Choosing such a path was not easy for his millions of followers, but, with Gandhi as its guide, the free nation of India was born.

Nonviolence was not a new idea, of course. Most great religions of the world preach against violence. However, people have tended to use these teachings only in their personal lives. Gandhi brought nonviolence into public life and used it to change governments and their laws. For Gandhi, nonviolence was not a sign of weakness—it was a way for people to become even stronger. It could also be a powerful force for change. Nonviolence could change laws, gain freedom and equal rights, and even sway entire nations.

THE GREAT SOUL

Gandhi's Hindu religion was the most important force in his life. He wasn't interested in having money or owning things because possessions got in the way of his spiritual life. It was

Gandhi was a small man, but his influence was enormous.

Indian writer Rabindranath Tagore, who gave the name Mahatma ("Great Soul") to Mohandas Gandhi

clear to everyone that Gandhi was truly a holy man. In fact, the Indian writer Rabindranath Tagore gave Gandhi the name Mahatma, which means "Great Soul."

Through his teachings and tireless efforts, Gandhi helped millions of people gain self-rule. The first step he taught was that self-rule begins with the individual, with oneself. People must learn to control their own feelings and desires. For Gandhi, that included the desire for food. Many times, he brought about changes by fasting—going without food for days or even weeks. It's no wonder that people saw him as a great soul.

CHANGING THE WORLD

Gandhi introduced many ideas to help bring about change without violence. One was **passive resistance**, which simply means doing nothing. If someone attacks, Gandhi said, just stay there without fighting back, and in time, the attacker will give up. Another idea was **civil disobedience**, which means disobeying or ignoring laws that are unfair. Yet another idea was the **boycott**. To boycott a business means to stop buying its products as a protest against its actions.

Gandhi helped to change people's minds about old ideas such as **colonialism**. In Gandhi's time, Great Britain was one of the world's most powerful nations, with an **empire** that included colonies all over the globe. The British liked to brag, saying, "The sun never sets on the British Empire." India had been under Great Britain's control since the 1700s. Now, Indians wanted self-rule—and with Gandhi as their leader, they got it. Soon people in colonies all over the world saw that freedom was not just a hopeless dream, and dozens of new nations were born as their people threw off colonial rule.

Gandhi also helped to wake people up about racism and equal rights. He taught that all human beings have the same rights, and many of the world's great freedom fighters learned from him. Among them were Nelson Mandela in South Africa and Martin Luther King Jr. in the United States. They used Gandhi's methods of passive resistance, civil disobedience, and boycotts to gain freedom for their followers. Indeed, nonviolence is as powerful today as it was in Gandhi's time. "Nonviolence is not a weapon of the weak," Gandhi said. "It is a weapon of the strongest and the bravest."

A large crowd listening to Gandhi in Calcutta

GROWING UP IN INDIA

Mohandas Karamchand Gandhi was born on October 2, 1869. His hometown was Porbandar, a small seaport on the western coast of India. Today, Porbandar is in the Indian state of Gujarat.

Little Mohan's parents were named Karamchand and Putlibai. Karamchand was an official in the local government. (Though India was a colony of Great Britain at that time, some local rule was allowed.) Karamchand had very little education, but he was good at his job. Putlibai was Karamchand's fourth wife. His previous wives had died, each leaving children behind, so Mohan lived in a large, extended family with many siblings. He was Putlibai's fourth child.

The town of Porbandar, Gandhi's birthplace

RELIGION AT HOME

Mohan's mother cared little about fancy clothes or jewelry. As a Hindu, Putlibai's religion was the most important part of her life. Day after day, Mohan watched his mother go to the temple to pray. He watched her refuse food on her many fasting days. And whenever friends or relatives were sick, Putlibai was there to care for them.

Mohan admired his mother's goodness. Putlibai followed a very devout form of **Hinduism**. Because she respected all living creatures, she was a **vegetarian**, eating no meat. In addition, she fasted to purify herself of the desire for food. Although her own faith was strong, Putlibai also respected people who held different beliefs. All his life, Mohan remembered his mother's devotion and tried to follow her example.

A Hindu temple in India

Hinduism

Hinduism is one of the oldest religions in the world, and it has many different forms. Some Hindus honor three principal gods—Brahma, Vishnu, and Shiva (in statue, right). Others honor only Brahma. Hindus may worship at small roadside shrines or in magnificent temples. The important Hindu value of *ahimsa* was the basis for Gandhi's teachings on nonviolence. Ahimsa means "doing no harm to any living creature." Today, more than 450 million people around the world practice Hinduism.

A Very Shy Boy

Gandhi wrote about his childhood:

I used to be very shy and avoided all company. My books and my lessons were my sole companions. To be at school at the stroke of the hour and to run back home as soon as the school closed—that was my daily habit. I literally ran back, because I could not bear to talk to anybody. I was even afraid lest anyone should poke fun at me.

SCHOOL DAYS—AND MARRIAGE

Porbandar was a poor town, and its schools were primitive. Mohan and the other schoolchildren wrote their letters in the dirt with their fingers. When he was seven, Mohan's family moved slightly east to Rajkot, a larger town with better schools. Although Mohan won school prizes now and then, he was not an outstanding student, nor was he much of an athlete. What Mohan enjoyed most was taking long walks alone in the countryside.

One day when he was thirteen years old, Mohan noticed a flurry of activity among his relatives. Soon he learned that one of his cousins was going to be married. The real shock, however, was yet to come. Mohan found that he was to be married too!

It was customary in India at that time for parents to arrange their children's marriages, a practice that is still followed in many parts of the nation today. Young people were often married at a very early age, and the husband and wife may never have met before their wedding day. As a result, at the age of thirteen, Mohan found himself married to a thirteen-year-old girl named Kasturba Makanji.

The Gandhi home in Rajkot

Married life was a little confusing for the young couple. After all, they were still children in many ways. Mohan often became jealous when he thought Kasturba was too friendly with others. He sometimes tried to control her with strict rules, but this didn't work very well. At the same time, Mohan was busy being a typical teenager, rebelling and getting into mischief. For instance, he secretly tried eating meat, which was of course forbidden by his religion. He was so sorry later that he vowed, "Never again!" Despite his rebelliousness, he loved reading religious stories about the great Hindu heroes, and he wanted to be like them.

Mohandas and Kasturba Gandhi were married very young and remained devoted to each other for many years.

DECIDING ON A FUTURE

When Mohan was still in high school, his father died. Soon Mohan took his college entrance exams, barely managing to pass. College turned out to be even harder than he had feared, mainly because Mohan spoke Gujarati—one of the many local languages in India—but all his classes were taught in English.

Next, he and his family began to plan his future. Mohan thought he might like to be a doctor, but that presented a problem. Cutting into the flesh of any creature—human or animal—was against his family's religion. So instead, he decided to follow in his father's footsteps and become a government official. To qualify for a government appointment, however, Mohan would have to become a lawyer. He would need to study law in England, a long ocean voyage away. With a heavy heart, he left behind his family—which now included an infant son.

CHAPTER 3

BECOMING A LAWYER

After weeks at sea, the young man arrived in London, England, one of the world's largest cities. He had never seen such a busy, bustling place, and it made his head spin! Horse-drawn carriages rumbled past, and he quickly learned to jump out of the way. He enrolled in the Inner Temple, one of London's fine law colleges. Now he was called "Mr. Gandhi."

London in the 1880s

NEW IDEAS

Before Gandhi left home, his mother had made him promise to stay away from three things while he was abroad—wine, women, and meat. Not eating meat turned out to be the hardest! New friends in London warned him that avoiding meat was not good for his health. He would become weak, they said, and wouldn't be able to study well.

In time, he met many other vegetarians in London. He even joined the London Vegetarian Society and became an outspoken leader. Gandhi had always been painfully shy, but now he began to come out of his shell.

Gandhi's English got better day by day. Hoping to become a proper gentleman, he took lessons in violin and in ballroom dancing. He also met people with exciting new ideas. Some wanted to change modern life and go back to simpler ways. Others taught him about different religions, such as Islam and Christianity. He began reading the Bible and the **Bhagavad-Gita**, a classic book about his own Hindu religion.

LOOKING FOR WORK

When Gandhi returned to India in 1891, he got a few shocks. His mother had died while he was away, and he discovered that he missed her terribly. Also, it was almost impossible for him to find a job. Gandhi looked for work in Bombay,

Life without Meat

About his time in London, Gandhi wrote:

The landlady was at a loss to know what [foods] to prepare for me. We had oatmeal porridge for breakfast, which was fairly filling, but I always starved at lunch and dinner. . . . Both for luncheon and dinner we had spinach and bread and jam, too. I was a good eater . . . but I was ashamed to ask for more than two or three slices of bread, as it did not seem correct to do so.

Gandhi as a young law student

13

Kasturba

Kasturba, or "Ba" as he called her, was Gandhi's wife from 1883 until her death in 1944. The couple had four sons—Harilal, Manilal, Ramdas, and Devadas. In India, Kasturba often worked closely with her husband, encouraging women to join the struggle for freedom. She was put in jail many times, just as Gandhi was. Gandhi was at Kasturba's bedside when she died.

one of India's major cities, but many other young lawyers were there too—so many that it seemed there were more lawyers than jobs. Gandhi even tried to get a part-time job teaching high school, but he was turned down. With a wife and a growing family to support (another son was born in 1892), he was becoming desperate.

Terror in the Courtroom

Gandhi wrote about his first court case:

I stood up, but my heart sank into my boots. My head was reeling and I felt as though the whole Court was doing likewise. I could think of no question to ask. The judge must have laughed. . . . But I was past seeing anything. I sat down and told the agent that I could not conduct the case. . . . I hastened from the Court, not knowing whether my client won or lost her case, but I was ashamed of myself, and decided not to take up any more cases until I had courage enough to conduct them.

The busy city of Bombay in 1891

Gandhi finally found some legal work, but things did not go well. On his first day in court, he was so nervous that he could hardly speak. In despair, he went back to the town of Rajkot, where his family lived. There he made a meager living writing legal papers. One day, a law firm offered him a one-year job in South Africa. It meant another long sea voyage, but Gandhi felt he couldn't say no.

STRUGGLES IN SOUTH AFRICA

Gandhi as a lawyer in 1906

Gandhi soon learned that many other Indians lived in South Africa. Like India, South Africa was a colony of Great Britain. The British and other Europeans belonged to the ruling class there, while Indians and blacks were treated as lower classes.

THE TRIP THAT CHANGED HIS LIFE

One day, Gandhi's boss asked him to take a long business trip that required him to travel by train and stagecoach from the city of Durban to Pretoria. On that journey, Gandhi experienced prejudice firsthand. On the train, soon after Gandhi settled into his first-class carriage, a European passenger complained to the conductor that an Indian was on board. Gandhi was asked to move to the baggage car, but he refused. The police came along at the next stop and threw him off the train, bags and all. Gandhi sat freezing in the railway station all night. "Should I fight for my rights, or go back to India?" he wondered. Many years later, Gandhi remembered this night as the turning point in his life.

For many years, people of color could ride in only third-class cars on South African trains.

People of South Africa

People of many cultures live in South Africa today. The Afrikaners are the descendants of settlers from the Netherlands, France, and Germany. They speak Afrikaans, a form of Dutch. Other whites, who speak English, are descended from British, Irish, or Scottish people. The ancestors of the Asian people came from India and Malaysia, and blacks are the country's native Africans. People of mixed race in South Africa are called Coloreds.

THE FREEDOM FIGHT BEGINS

Every day in South Africa, Gandhi saw more prejudice against Indians and other ethnic groups. As his year in South Africa was coming to an end, his Indian friends gave him a going-away party where he heard some bad news. The state of Natal, where he was living, was about to pass a new law that would ban all Indians from voting. His friends begged him to stay and help them defeat

British forces in Pretoria during the Boer War

the passage of the new law, and of course Gandhi felt he could not refuse. Gandhi quickly organized his fellow Indians. He made speeches, wrote letters, and gathered hundreds of followers, but the law passed anyway. Natal's Indians lost the right to vote.

Gandhi was just getting started, however. He formed the Natal Indian Congress to organize Indians and teach them about their rights. Besides voting rights, he said, they should have good jobs, education, and health care. Because of his activities, he was quickly getting to be known to government officials as a troublemaker. Meanwhile, newspapers in India, Britain, and other countries were writing about his fight for Indians' rights. The embarrassing news about prejudice in British colonies was spreading around the world.

Gandhi returned to India in 1896 to collect his family. When he, Kasturba, and their two sons got back to South Africa, an angry mob of white citizens attacked Gandhi. Still, he kept doing his work. Since he firmly believed in working within the law instead of breaking it, he repeatedly made official complaints to the government about Indians' lack of rights.

Kindness and service to others were always important to Gandhi. During South Africa's Boer War between the British and the Dutch, which began in 1899, he even helped the British side by organizing more than one thousand Indians to provide medical services. But despite his efforts and no matter how hard he tried, conditions were not improving for South Africa's Indians.

SATYAGRAHA

By 1906, Gandhi decided it was time to do things in a different way. He called his new policy *satyagraha*, which means "holding onto the truth." If a law was unjust—if it was based on untruth—then people should disobey it. This is also called civil disobedience. For Gandhi, it was a way to fight without being violent. Gandhi set strict rules for anyone conducting a satyagraha. The person had to be prepared to accept any results, such as losing a job or going to jail. Also, the person should respect his or her enemies, keep an open mind about their ideas, and try to solve problems in a peaceful way.

For the next seven years, Gandhi's followers used satyagraha against many anti-Indian laws. Hundreds of Indians lost their jobs, went to jail, or were beaten. Gandhi himself was jailed for a time, but even then he practiced what he preached. While in jail, he made a pair of sandals for a government leader.

Meeting "the Saint"

General Jan Christiaan Smuts (above) was a South African leader who once met with Gandhi to try to work out an agreement. While Gandhi was in jail, he made sandals for Smuts. When Gandhi finally left South Africa, Smuts said, "The saint has left our shores—I hope forever."

CHAPTER 5

RISING AS A LEADER IN INDIA

Gandhi returned to his homeland of India in 1915. By now he was committed to helping his people and ready for the task. His years in South Africa had made him a strong leader.

In the Indian state of Bihar, Gandhi helped farm-workers get better working conditions. Then he helped workers in a cloth factory in Ahmadabad. This time, he got his way by fasting. The factory owners didn't want him to starve, so they gave in to his demands.

Gandhi's words were read and heard all over the world.

THE AMRITSAR MASSACRE

The whole nation of India heard about Gandhi in 1919. That year, India's British leaders passed the Rowlatt Bills. These laws targeted people who held demonstrations against the government and said the organizers were to be jailed without a trial.

Gandhi declared a nationwide satyagraha to protest the Rowlatt Bills. As always, he called for nonviolent resistance. He asked Indians to go on strike—to refuse to go to work. As a result, businesses across the country shut down. When Gandhi was arrested in the state of Punjab, riots broke out. In the city of Amritsar, British soldiers shot into an angry crowd, killing almost four hundred people.

Police trying to control a demonstration in India

Gandhi Speaks

Gandhi's well-known statements include the following:

"Where there is love, there is life."

"What you do is of little significance. But it is very important that you do it."

"Prayer is the key of the morning and the bolt of the evening."

"I would dance with joy if I had to give up politics."

"What is faith worth if it is not translated into action?"

"I believe in equality for everyone, except reporters and photographers."

Mahatma Gandhi and other members of the Indian National Congress

Now, more than ever before, Gandhi wanted to free India from the British. He began preaching a policy of noncooperation, asking Indians not to take part in any British organizations, including businesses, schools, courts, and government agencies. The British owned most large companies, so Gandhi urged people to start small home industries, such as spinning and weaving. He wanted Indians to learn to rely on themselves.

THE GREAT TRIAL

Gandhi helped Indians gain power through an organization called the Indian National Congress (INC). Little by little, the Indian people were beginning to see that they did not need to live under British rule. Unfortunately, not everyone kept Gandhi's rules against violence. In 1922, for example, a mob of Indians attacked British policemen, killing twenty-one men. Deeply saddened, Gandhi fasted for five days in honor of the dead. Then he was arrested and charged with crimes against the government. His trial came to be called the Great Trial. In the crowded courtroom, Gandhi made powerful speeches against British rule. All eyes were on him— not just in India, but around the world. In spite of his passionate, eloquent words, he was sentenced to six years in jail.

Gandhi leading a Salt March in 1930 to protest the government's policy

THE SALT ACTS

Prison did nothing to change Gandhi's mind about independence for India. In 1930, after his release from jail, he decided to protest the Salt Acts. Under these laws, only the government could sell salt. Since salt taxes were very high, this was a hardship on India's poorest people.

Gandhi led a crowd of followers to the seashore. He reached down, picked up a lump of natural sea salt, and held it up for all to see. This was his way of telling people to break the salt laws. Gandhi's action violated the law because he was making use of nongovernment salt. Soon, demonstrations and civil disobedience swept the nation, and about sixty thousand Indians were jailed,

Gandhi's followers evaporating seawater to get salt—a violation of the Salt Acts

The Caste System

The Hindu **caste system** has five major levels. At the top are the **Brahmans** (above), the priests and scholars. Next are the **Rajanyas**, or political leaders. Then there are the **Vaishyas**, the merchants and artisans. Beneath them are the **Sudras**, or servants. Finally, at the bottom level, are the Panchamas, or **Untouchables**.

including Gandhi. Gandhi had hoped the salt protest would force the British to give Indians their independence. When this too failed, he tried to help the poor of India in other ways.

Untouchables did the most menial jobs.

CHILDREN OF GOD

In the Hindu religion, people are born into castes, or classes. For many years, the lowest class was called the "Untouchables." This term implied that these people were never to be in contact with the higher classes. Gandhi had worked to help India's Untouchables, who had almost no rights or protections under the law. Gandhi gave them the name "children of God" and fasted several times to force the country to change its policies toward Untouchables. Slowly, things began to change. Today, the constitution forbids unequal treatment of any of its citizens, but some discrimination does remain.

CHAPTER 6

BUILDING A NATION FROM THE BOTTOM UP

In 1934, Gandhi moved to the tiny village of Sevagram, far from big-city life. There he founded the All India Village Industries Association—a group that taught village people how to make a living by working at home.

Under Gandhi's leadership, villagers learned crafts of all kinds.

Villagers learned spining and weaving cloth, making paper, breeding cattle, and many other skills. They also learned to read and to prevent diseases. Gandhi called this "building a nation from the bottom up."

HINDUS AND MUSLIMS

Meanwhile, India was moving closer to independence, but many problems remained. While most Indians belonged to the Hindu religion, a large part of the population were **Muslims**, who followed the faith of Islam. And many of India's Muslims wanted a separate nation for themselves.

Village Industries

Spinning and weaving cloth was an important industry in India, so Gandhi encouraged it. The spinning wheel became a symbol of village industries, and pictures of Gandhi often show him sitting at a spinning wheel. Gandhi also trained people in pottery-making, oil-pressing, beekeeping, cattle-raising, and working with leather.

Gandhi believed in a unified India. All his life, he had preached cooperation, tolerance, and respect for others. He felt that a divided India would be a weaker India. Again and again, he persuaded Hindu and Muslim leaders to join hands and work together. Nevertheless, their cooperation remained very shaky.

TRADING WAR FOR INDEPENDENCE

In World War II (1939–1945), Great Britain and other nations fought against Germany, Japan, and Italy. As a British colony, India went to war as well.

This posed a serious issue for Gandhi, since for him, nonviolence was the only way to resolve conflicts. He and his faithful followers were against war. However, many members of the INC were not as committed to peace and pacifism as Gandhi was. They saw the war as a chance to gain independence. The INC tried to bargain with India's British leaders. If you give us independence, they said, we will go to war for you.

Indian soldiers during World War II

Gandhi was brokenhearted. This was not the way he had taught people to live. Now he used all his energy to call for independence—his way.

QUIT INDIA!

In 1942, Gandhi launched the "Quit India" campaign to force the British to leave. He called for all Indians to practice civil disobedience and nonviolent resistance. This time, he asked that they "do or die"—that is, he asked that they should struggle to the death if necessary.

Sadly, violence broke out all over India, and Gandhi was blamed for it. He and most of the INC leaders were imprisoned for two years. Gandhi, in poor health, was released in 1944. This was to be his last imprisonment. He had spent a total of 2,338 days of his life in jail.

Meanwhile, the Muslim League in India supported the British side and gained more power. After World War II ended in 1945, talks about independence began again. Now it was a three-way talk involving the British rulers, INC leaders, and the Muslim League. People around the country were in an uproar. Hindu and Muslim groups, full of anger and prejudice, were rioting against each other. Gandhi traveled from one region to another, begging for peace and goodwill.

THE PRICE OF INDEPENDENCE

At last, in 1947, the three sides agreed. Britain would leave, and India would become free and independent. Gandhi's friend Jawaharlal Nehru would become **prime minister** of the new India. However, the country would be split into two separate nations—India for the Hindus and Pakistan for the Muslims.

Jawaharlal Nehru

Jawaharlal Nehru (1889–1964) was a strong and popular leader in India. He joined Gandhi's push for independence after the bloody Amritsar Massacre in 1919. Like Gandhi, Nehru (above left) had been put in jail many times. In 1929, he became president of the INC. Nehru was India's first prime minister after independence. He was often called Pandit, which means "Teacher."

Muslims leaving India for a new life in Pakistan, 1947

This was one of the saddest moments of Gandhi's life. He had met his goal of independence for India, but the price was a divided country. He had failed to bring all Indians together in peace.

The Hindu-Muslim Riots

Pakistan became an independent nation on August 14, 1947, and India gained its independence the day after. This division was accompanied by riots and bloodshed. Hindus fled from Pakistan into India, while Muslims in India fled to Pakistan. During this period of unrest, about half a million people were killed. Such violence was exactly what Gandhi had spent his life preaching against.

A GREAT SOUL TO THE VERY END

Even after independence, peace was still Gandhi's principal goal. Many Hindus and Muslims were angry about the way India had been carved up, and they blamed Gandhi for it. Some Hindus thought he had given away too much to the Muslims, and some Muslims felt they had not been given enough. Violent riots were flaring up everywhere. In the major city of Calcutta, Gandhi brought peace in his usual nonviolent way—by fasting. Next he went to Delhi, capital of the new India.

Mahatma Gandhi during one of his many fasts

The Indian city of Delhi

opposite: Leaving a prayer meeting; this is believed to be the last photo taken of Gandhi before he was killed.

THE LAST DAY

Gandhi arose at 3:30 a.m. on Friday, January 30, 1948. Things were still tense in Delhi, where Gandhi had just finished a six-day fast. As a result of his fast, warring groups had agreed to set aside their differences for a while. That evening, Gandhi was scheduled to lead an outdoor meeting in prayers for peace.

After his morning prayers, Gandhi spent his day writing letters and documents. He met with an official of India's new government. Then visitors from all over India lined up to speak with him. They asked his advice on politics, religion, and personal problems. One little girl asked for his autograph. Finally it was time to leave for the prayer meeting.

Gandhi had trouble walking alone. He was seventy-eight years old and was still weak from fasting. His grand-nieces, Abha and Manu, held his arms as he walked to the prayer grounds. About five hundred people were gathered there for Gandhi's evening prayers.

Nathuram Godse, the man who killed Gandhi

MURDER AT THE PRAYER MEETING

People cleared a path for the beloved old man as he passed. Many bowed down, some bowing as low as his feet. Soon he reached the wooden stage and climbed the five steps up to the top. Then he turned and gave the traditional Hindu greeting, putting his hands together and holding them high.

Suddenly, a young man rushed forward. Manu tried to hold him back, but he knocked her down. Standing right in front of Gandhi, he pulled out a pistol and fired three shots. Within minutes, the old man was dead. His killer was Nathuram Godse, a Hindu extremist who believed Gandhi had hurt India by associating with Muslims.

Gandhi had always hoped to die with the name of God on his lips. True to his wishes, his last words were "He Ram, He Ram" ("Oh God, Oh God"). He died as he had lived—as a Mahatma, a Great Soul.

THEY FOLLOWED HIS PATH

Gandhi's life and death touched people's hearts around the world, and his lessons in nonviolence lived on long after him. He became a shining example to all who hoped for freedom and equal rights.

One person deeply influenced by him was the black South African leader Nelson Mandela, who admired Gandhi's work with South Africa's Indians. Mandela tried to use Gandhi's methods to gain equal rights for his nation's blacks. Mandela spent twenty-eight years in prison, but South Africa's blacks finally won their rights in 1993.

opposite: A large crowd of people at the memorial where Gandhi's ashes were placed

Gandhi also inspired the U.S. **civil rights** leader Martin Luther King Jr. In the 1950s and 1960s, Dr. King worked to gain equal rights for African-Americans. He admired Gandhi and urged his followers to use nonviolence. Eventually, King's leadership led to the passing of the Civil Rights Act of 1964.

Arun Gandhi (seen here with his wife, Sumanda) continues the work of his grandfather.

DESCENDANTS OF GREAT MEN

Arun Gandhi is the grandson of Mahatma Gandhi, and Martin Luther King III is the son of Dr. King. Today, both men are working together to spread the message of nonviolence and equal rights. Arun Gandhi has explained their feelings this way:

"Although both [Gandhi and King] lived at different times, there was a spiritual bond between the two and we must honor that spiritual bond. Both shared the same dream that people would live in peace and harmony without looking at each other's differences."

Nelson Mandela

Nelson Mandela (1918–) led many protests against South Africa's **apartheid** (separation of races) laws. Inspired by Gandhi, he urged nonviolent action. Even from jail, he inspired blacks in their struggle. Mandela was awarded the Nobel Peace Prize in 1993. In 1994, he became the first black president of South Africa.

Dr. Martin Luther King Jr.

Dr. Martin Luther King Jr. (1929–1968) was a Baptist minister who led the African-American civil rights movement. In **theological seminary**, he learned about Mahatma Gandhi and his teachings on nonviolence. He followed these ideas as he fought for equal rights. King (shown here wearing a cap, leading a civil rights march) won the Nobel Peace Prize in 1964. Like Gandhi, King was imprisoned many times. His life ended in Memphis, Tennessee, when he was shot and killed.

King explained his impressions of Gandhi this way:

Gandhi was inevitable. If humanity is to progress, Gandhi is inescapable. He lived, thought and acted, inspired by the vision of humanity evolving toward a world of peace and harmony. We may ignore Gandhi at our own risk.

TIMELINE

1869	Mohandas Gandhi is born on October 2 in Porbandar, India
1876	Moves to Rajkot with his family
1883	Is married at age thirteen to Kasturba Makanji
1888	Sails to England to study law
1891	Begins practicing law in India
1893	Takes a job in South Africa
1903	Opens law office in Johannesberg, South Africa
1906	Organizes his first protest against anti-Indian laws in South Africa
1908	Is imprisoned in South Africa
1915	Returns to India
1922	After Great Trial, is sentenced to six years in jail
1930	Goes to jail for breaking India's Salt Laws
1932	Begins fasting to protest treatment of Untouchables
1934	Launches the All India Village Industries Association
1942	Begins the nationwide "Quit India" movement
1944	His wife, Kasturba, dies at age seventy-four
1947	India gains independence but is divided into two countries
1948	Is shot dead on January 30 at a prayer meeting in Delhi

ahimsa: doing no harm to any living creature

apartheid: a separation of races once practiced in South Africa

Bhagavad-Gita: a sacred book of the Hindu religion

boycott: the act of not using a service or buying a product as a form of protest

Brahmans: priests and scholars at the top of the Hindu caste system

caste system: a system of social classes into which people are born

civil disobedience: ignoring unfair laws

civil rights: basic equal rights for all citizens

colonialism: a system in which a nation controls a group of people in another nation

empire: a number of countries ruled by the same leader

Hinduism: a religious philosophy followed by many people in India

Muslims: people who follow Islam, the religion based on the teachings of Muhammad

passive resistance: a form of protest that involves noncooperation

prime minister: title given to the person in charge of the government in India, Great Britain, and some other countries

Rajanyas: political leaders in the Hindu caste system

satyagraha: a policy set by Gandhi that literally means "holding onto the truth"; according to this policy, if a law is unjust, a person should practice civil disobedience and refuse to obey that law

Sudras: servants in the Hindu caste system

theological seminary: a religious school where people study to become ministers, priests, or rabbis

Untouchables: members of the lowest class in the Hindu caste system

Vaishyas: merchants and artisans in the Hindu caste system

vegetarian: someone who chooses not to eat meat

TO FIND OUT MORE

BOOKS

Bains, Rae. *Gandhi, Peaceful Warrior.* New York: Troll, 1990.

Barraclough, John. *Mohandas Gandhi* (Lives and Times). Crystal Lake, Ill.: Heineman Library, 1997.

Malaspina, Ann. *Mahatma Gandhi and India's Independence in World History* (In World History). Springfield, N.J.: Enslow Publishers, 2000.

Martin, Christopher. *Mohandas Gandhi* (A&E Biography). Minneapolis, Minn.: Lerner Publications Company, 2000.

Mitchell, Pratima. *Gandhi: The Father of Modern India* (What's Their Story). New York: Oxford University Press, 1998.

INTERNET SITES

ABCNews.Com
http://archive.abcnews.go.com/sections/world/gandhi/gandhi_photoessay.html
A photo essay on the life of Gandhi.

The History of Hinduism
http://www.hinduismtoday.kauai.hi.us/Resources/TimeLine/HinduHistory.html
Gives the history of the Hindu religion from its earliest times.

Mahatma Gandhi
http://www.sscnet.ucla.edu/southasia/History/Gandhi/gandhi.html
Offers a short biography of Gandhi, plus information about his wife and the history of India.

Mahatma Gandhi's Last Days
http://www.itihaas.com/modern/gandhilastdays.html
Tells how Gandhi spent the last few days of his life.

M. K. Gandhi Institute for Nonviolence Website
http://www.gandhiinstitute.org/aboutmkg.html
A resource for information about Gandhi and his philosophy of nonviolence. It includes quotes and a photo library.

The Official Mahatma Gandhi Website
http://www.mahatma.org.in/audio.jsp?link=bg
Includes the complete text of his autobiography and a page with many of his quotations.

TIME.com
http://www.time.com/time/time100/poc/quiz3.html
A brief quiz about Gandhi's life.

INDEX

About the Author

Ann Heinrichs grew up in Fort Smith, Arkansas. She began playing the piano at age three and thought she would grow up to be a pianist. Instead, she became a writer. Now she has written more than forty books for children and young adults. Several of her books have won national awards. Ms. Heinrichs now lives in Chicago, Illinois. She enjoys martial arts and traveling to countries throughout the world.